MW01488629

# Overcoming Overwhelmed Workbook

*Don't Crack Under the Pressure*

**To Be Used With the Overcoming Overwhelmed Book or Bible Study**

By Pastor Erik Lawson

Copyright @ 2022 by 415 Leadership.

All rights reserved. No part of this book may be reproduced, stored, or transmitted by any means— whether auditory, graphic, mechanical, or electronic—without written permission of both publisher and author, except in the case of brief excerpts used in critical articles and reviews. Unauthorized reproduction of any part of this work is illegal and punishable by law.

Because of the dynamic nature of the Internet, any web addresses or links contained in this book may have changed since publication and may no longer be valid.

Workbook ISBN-13: 979-8-9868682-3-3

Paperback ISBN-13: 979-8-9868682-1-9

eBook (Kindle) ISBN-13: 979-8-9868682-2-6


First edition published in 2022.
Published in the United States.

Visit the author's website at: www.eriklawson.com

Published by 415 Leadership Inc.
100 Mall Parkway, Suite 500
Wentzville, Missouri 63385

# Table of Contents

# Overcoming Overwhelmed

# Introduction

*Then Jesus said, "Come to me, all of you who are weary and carry heavy burdens, and I will give you rest. Take my yoke upon you. Let me teach you, because I am humble and gentle at heart, and you will find rest for your souls. For my yoke is easy to bear, and the burden I give you is light." Matthew 11:28-30 (New Living Translation)*

First, He tells us to "Come to Him."

Second, He tells us to "take His yoke."

Third, He asks us to "Let me teach you."

This workbook was designed to be used in conjunction with the book **Overcoming Overwhelmed**. In this workbook, for each chapter of the book, I've included many of the most memorable quotes and Scriptures. To reinforce the chapter theme, you'll find a **Connect with His Word** Bible reading assignment that will reinforce the truth found in the chapter along with a **One Minute Devotional**, which will be indicated with the 1-minute picture.

Also, for each chapter, there is a **Marker Moment and a Look Back.**

**Marker Moments** are designed to help you reflect on your own life in light of the topic. These will help you apply the principles to your own life in a practical way. Keep this where it can be easily found and reviewed.

**Set a reminder** on your phone or calendar at the end of each **Marker Moment.** You'll be reminded to set a reminder to go back and do the Look Back moment.

There is also a **Prayer of Commitment** section to reinforce your commitment to yourself and help you when you may struggle.

 You'll find the **Look Back** section immediately after the **Marker Moment** in each chapter. This is where you can literally **look back** to see how the changes you have made have impacted your life and the lives of those in your circle of influence over time. You'll want to make notes of the improvements for the future look backs. **We tend to leak with time, and sometimes we need a refill to get back on track. This workbook can act as an oasis for a spiritual refill.** I encourage you, don't just look back one time. Make it a habit to look back from time to time to see your continual progress. **Change is a process, not an event.**

| |
|---|
| **Change is a process, not an event.** |

# SECTION 1

# OVERCOMING
# OVERWHELM

# Chapter 1

# Overwhelmed by Busy

## Connect with His Word

John 1 NLT, Romans 10

## One Minute Devotional

 This is a world filled with busy. If you don't believe me, ask yourself what your most common answer is when someone asks you how you've been. I'd be willing to bet most of the time it is a one-word answer, "busy." We are all scrambling looking for ultimately one thing, significance. There is only one source for true significance, and it doesn't come from a job, social status, or wealth. It can only be found in Jesus.

*"But to all who believed him and accepted him, he gave the right to become children of God. They are reborn—not with a physical birth resulting from human passion or plan, but a birth that comes from God." John 1:12-13 (NLT)*

If our relationship with Jesus isn't the foundation of our life and our identity is not in Him, we will continually be spinning our proverbial wheels picking up unnecessary weights in the vain attempt to find fulfillment. If you have not made that commitment to Christ, or have walked away from Him, I can't encourage you enough to take that step to commit or recommit your life to Him. (There is a prayer you can say at the end of Chapter 1 if you would like to do that.) I promise this is the best first step you can ever take. There's no way to describe the joy of becoming a new creation in Christ until you experience it for yourself. As a bonus, you will find as you get your life in order that much of your stress will self-correct.

## We pack unnecessary weights.

What unnecessary weights have you been carrying?

_____

_____

_____

_____

# Busy because of lack of purpose.

**Often, the reason we fail in our relationships is because we're busy giving the best part of ourselves to things that don't matter.**

What is most important to you in your life? What are you giving most of your time and energy to? Are these things in alignment with what is most important in your life?

_____

_____

_____

_____

_____

_____

> **God has created you for a life of significance, not a life of busy.**

Would you describe your current life as one of significance, or are you just busy? Why did you answer this way?

_____

_____

_____

_____

_____

_____

> **Jesus already defined my worth and there is nothing I can do that makes me more valuable.**

*"For in Him dwells all the fullness of the Godhead bodily; and you are complete in Him, who is the head of all principality and power." Colossians 2:9-10 (New King James Version)*

Be honest with yourself, do you believe this? Or, do you think success or achievements or just being involved in a lot of activities will add to your value? Why do you think this? Where did this idea first come from? Does it still serve you?

_____

_____

_____

_____

_____

_____

LIFE IS MEASURED BY MOMENTS

## Marker Moment

In this chapter, we looked at how we get overwhelmed with busy and gained some perspective as to why we fall into the busy trap. We discovered that "too busy" is a symptom of misplaced priorities and a misbelief that busy adds to your value as a person. The bottom line is, we are all looking for significance in our lives, but the truth is, significance is only found in Jesus.

For some of us, we say "yes" to the wrong things and people. For others, busy is almost a status symbol, it makes us feel important.

I think we can all relate to getting to the end of a very busy day and thinking, "What did I do today?" We had activity with little or no progress.

We also saw that being overly busy can spill into our significant relationships with damaging effects.

Most importantly, we discovered that accepting Jesus as our Lord and Savior is the most important step you will take toward a life of significance.

Take a moment and have an honest conversation with yourself, have you fallen into the trap of "too busy?"

1. Look over your calendar, is it filled with activities that have no eternal value? Note ones here that you can eliminate to make more margin for the things that really matter in your life.

_____

_____

_____

_____

_____

When will you commit to do that? On (date): _____.

2. Have you been trying to get your identity from something other than Jesus? How?

_____

_____

_____

_____

_____

3. How can you change that?

_____

_____

_____

_____

_____

When will you commit to do that? On (date): _____.

If you prayed the prayer at the end of the chapter in the book, record the date here: _____.

**Set a reminder** on your phone or calendar for yourself for either 30 or 60 days from today, to remind yourself to pause and look back on how implementing these changes have impacted your life and the lives of those you care about the most.

# Prayer of Commitment

Father, forgive me for trying to get my identity from anything but You, and for filling my life with busy. I thank You that You love me unconditionally and that there is nothing I can do to make You love me more or less than You do right now. Help me to always keep my eyes on You and remind me when I allow busy to distract me from the things of eternal value in my life. I thank you for this. In Jesus' Name. Amen.

## Look Back

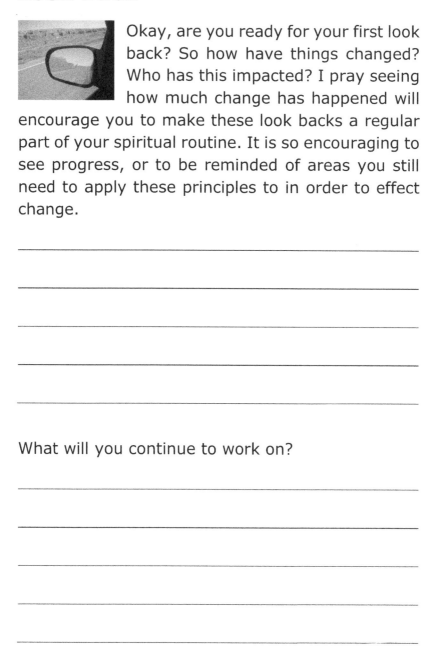 Okay, are you ready for your first look back? So how have things changed? Who has this impacted? I pray seeing how much change has happened will encourage you to make these look backs a regular part of your spiritual routine. It is so encouraging to see progress, or to be reminded of areas you still need to apply these principles to in order to effect change.

_____

_____

_____

_____

What will you continue to work on?

_____

_____

_____

_____

# Chapter 2

# Misbeliefs About Busy

## Connect with His Word

Psalm 91, Jeremiah 29:11-13

## One Minute Devotional

Today, I want to take a minute to encourage you with some life altering ways to use the scriptures that you just read. Psalm 91 was written by King David and is a great tool for both your peace of mind and as a weapon in your spiritual arsenal. According to Mirriam-Webster, a psalm is "a sacred song or poem used in worship, *especially* one of the biblical hymns collected in the Book of Psalms." By this definition, when you speak a Psalm out loud, it is actually a form of worship. I pray Psalm 91 over myself every day and I encourage you to do the same.

Jeremiah 29:11-13 tells you about God's plan for your life and how to find it. I encourage you to commit these verses to memory. Write these verses down in a way you can keep it in front of you often.

It can be on a 3x5 card that you keep in your wallet or tape to your mirror, or you can put it in your phone and review it often. The Scriptures are not just words on paper or on a screen, they are living words from the Creator of the Universe, a love letter sent to you.

*Misbelief #1: Busier is Easier.*

> *"The plans of the diligent lead to profit as surely as haste leads to poverty."* Proverbs 21:5 (New International Version)

**Everyone else has a plan for your life; shouldn't you also have one for your life?**

Is there an area of your life where you are missing a plan? What is it?

_____

_____

_____

_____

_____

*Misbelief #2: Busy is avoidance.*

> **We are a culture where people who've bought into the idea that if we stay busy enough, the truth of our lives won't catch up with us.**

What truth are you trying to out-run?

_____

_____

_____

_____

_____

_____

> **The real problem with this is, many of us are running from what God is trying to fix inside of us, because we have to feel to heal.**

*Misbelief #3: Busy feels good.*

> **Busy does not mean progress.**

Where are you spinning your wheels?

_____

_____

_____

_____

_____

_____

LIFE IS MEASURED BY MOMENTS

# Marker Moment

In Misbeliefs About Busy, we looked at how much easier it seems to just stay busy and go with the proverbial flow. This is a just let life come at you as it happens philosophy. However, we found that this is a very costly approach in the long run and one of the quickest paths to failure.

We also observed some of the harmful, if not devastating, effects that "too busy" can have in your life. If you've been taking the easy way out and you've been using avoidance as a tactic, in any area of your life, I encourage you to STOP. Take some time and ask God to show you, and what He'd like you to do about it. Lighten your load and I guarantee you you'll get your life back.

Finally, we discovered that busy can feel good, yet it doesn't always represent progress.

*1. To be honest, I've kept myself crazy busy to avoid . . . Make a list.*

_____

_____

_____

_____

_____

What steps can you take to change that?

_____

_____

_____

_____

MONTH _____ YEAR _____

Date action taken: _____.

Date action taken: _____.

Date action taken: _____.

*2. Which are you a bee or a mosquito? _____ Would you consider taking an electronics fast? _____*

MONTH _____ YEAR _____

*Date: _____.*

*From when to when? _____.*

**Set your reminder** again for 30 or 60 days after you've implemented these changes so you can reflect on the results of making these changes.

## Prayer of Commitment

Father, forgive me for the areas of my life that I've been taking the easy way out. I ask You to speak to my heart and show me any area where I have been using being busy to avoid doing those things that are best. Help me to be the bee and make a difference in my world. In Jesus' Name. Amen.

## Look Back

When you get your reminder, look back over this section and reflect on the changes you've seen since implementing these changes. How has this changed things in your life? Record those changes here.

_____

_____

_____

_____

_____

What will you continue to work on?

_____

_____

_____

_____

_____

_____

# Chapter 3

# The Growth Principle

## Connect with His Word

Genesis 22, Ephesians 2

## One Minute Devotional

 In Ephesians 2, God tells us that we are His masterpiece. Have your ever felt like anything but a masterpiece, especially when you're in the middle of a trial? The enemy's goal is to get your eyes on the trial and off His Word—which tells you who God says you are and who He is in your life. Abraham gives us a fresh perspective on the problems and trials of your life. In today's Bible reading, Abraham provides us with a beautiful picture of the faithfulness of God in what seems like a hopeless situation. Jesus is the same, yesterday, today, and forever. If He was faithful to Abraham, He will be faithful to you—if you put your trust in Him. He wants to be your Jehovah-Jireh today and every day.

*"For we are God's masterpiece. He has created us anew in Christ Jesus, so we can do the good things he planned for us long ago." Ephesians 2:10 (NLT)*

Be honest with yourself, do you see yourself as God's masterpiece? Why or why not? Where do you think this belief system developed? Is it consistent with God's Word? If not, which do you prefer to believe—your belief, or God's Word? Are you ready to surrender to His Word?

_____

_____

_____

_____

_____

_____

*1. God will be your Jehovah Jireh - Your Provider.*

*"Then He said, "Take now your son, your only son Isaac, whom you love, and go to the land of Moriah, and offer him there as a burnt offering on one of the mountains of which I shall tell you." Genesis 22:2 (NKJV)*

What dark hour have you faced that ended up being a blessing in disguise?

_____

_____

_____

_____

_____

*2. You Will Learn to Soar.*

> *"But those who wait on the Lord*
> *Shall renew their strength;*
> *They shall mount up with wings like eagles,*
> *They shall run and not be weary,*
> *They shall walk and not faint." Isaiah 40:31 (NKJV)*

What trial have you faced that made you stronger on the other side?

_____

_____

_____

_____

> **You don't renew your strength waiting on an answer. You renew your strength waiting on Jesus.**

Are you waiting on the answer, or are you waiting on Jesus? Are you willing to receive His answer, even if it is different than you expect? Do you trust Him that much?

_____

_____

_____

_____

_____

_____

> **You'll never experience all God has for you in the safety of the nest.**

What is one area you've allowed fear to stop you from getting out of the proverbial nest?

_____

_____

_____

_____

_____

_____

> **It's not about getting more done, it's about getting more of the right things done in our life.**

*"Come to Me, all you who labor and are heavy laden, and I will give you rest."* Matthew 11:28 (NKJV)

*"Take My yoke upon you and learn from Me, for I am gentle and lowly in heart, and you will find rest for your souls."* Matthew 11:29 (NKJV)

*3. When you're in the yoke with Jesus, He carries most of the load.*

> **Jesus loves you enough to let you fail so you can see that you are yoked to the wrong thing.**

When was a time when you looked back and saw that Jesus allowed you to fall down and skin your knees metaphorically, so that you could see you were going the wrong way?

_____

_____

_____

_____

_____

_____

_____

**LIFE IS MEASURED BY MOMENTS**

## Marker Moment

In this chapter, we discovered that problems are often the sandpaper God uses to smooth off our rough edges to produce the masterpiece He sees in us. We found three hidden benefits of problems. We saw from the life of Abraham that in the midst of your troubles, God will be your Jehovah Jireh, your provider. We learned that when you respond in trust to your problems, they will actually lift you higher and ultimately, you'll learn to soar in spite of them, or because of them.

This chapter also revealed an important lesson about the difference between waiting on an answer and waiting on the Lord. That exhaustion might be a symptom that you're yoked to the wrong thing. When you're in the yoke with Jesus your load gets a whole lot lighter.

*1. Is there an Isaac in your life that God is asking you to put on the altar? What is it?*

_____

_____

_____

_____

_____

_____

MONTH                    YEAR

When will you commit to do that? On (date): _____.

I put this on the altar: _____.

*2. Are there answers you are waiting on? What are they?*

_____

_____

_____

_____

_____

How can you wait on Jesus instead?

_____

_____

_____

_____

_____


*3. Are there burdens you're trying to carry alone? List them here.*

_____

_____

_____

_____

_____


MONTH _____ YEAR _____

I turned these over to the Lord on (date): _____.

4. Are you yoked to something besides Jesus? What?

_____

_____

_____

_____

_____

What steps will you make to change that?

_____

_____

_____

_____

_____

**Set a reminder** on your phone or calendar to notify yourself to look back one month after you've implemented these changes.

## Prayer of Commitment

Father, thank You that I am Your masterpiece, even if I don't feel like one. I choose to believe Your Word over what I feel. Thank You for sanding my  rough edges off so that I can become all You created me to be. Help me to see Your hand in troubles and to completely put my trust in You. May I always see You as Jehovah Jireh in my life. Remind me to stay in the yoke with You and to allow You to carry most of the weight. I thank You for this in Jesus' Name. Amen.

## Look Back

 Look back over these pages and reflect on the changes you have seen. Be sure to take time to express your gratitude to God.

_____

_____

_____

_____

_____

What will you continue to work on?

_____

_____

_____

_____

_____

_____

# Chapter 4

# The Perspective Principle

## Connect with His Word

Ephesians 2, Philippians 4

## One Minute Devotional

 If you're anything like me there have been days, or even weeks and months, or in some cases years, where you are so overwhelmed by your circumstances that you can't see the forest for the trees. As humans, it's just natural to equate your circumstances with reality, because they feel so real. However, when you get God's perspective on your circumstances, it is a game changer. Ephesians 2 shows you how to see things from God's perspective, because it tells you that you are already seated in heavenly places. From this perspective it is easier to see your circumstances more clearly. In Philippians 4 we learn from Paul that joy has nothing to do with circumstances. Our joy in found in Him. Nehemiah 8:10 tells us the joy of the Lord is your strength. If the devil can steal your joy, he has also stolen your strength. Ask God to show you your circumstances from His perspective. I promise, it may not change what you're going through, but it will change how you see your circumstances.

## Overwhelmed By Circumstances

*"...I want you to know, brethren, that the things which happened to me have actually turned out for the furtherance of the gospel..." Philippians 1:12 (NKJV)*

Can you think of a time in retrospect when something you thought was tragic in the moment turned out to be a blessing in disguise in the end? Jot down what happened as a reminder for the next time a negative circumstance comes your way.

_____

_____

_____

_____

_____

*"All the saints greet you, but especially those who are of Caesar's household."* Philippians 4:22 (NKJV)

> **Paul didn't let his circumstances dictate the level of his joy, because he was too focused on Jesus to let his circumstances affect his emotions.**

*"And behold, the Lord stood above it and said: "I am the Lord God of Abraham your father and the God of Isaac; the land on which you lie I will give to you and your descendants. Also, your descendants shall be as the dust of the earth; you shall spread abroad to the west and the east, to the north and the south; and in you and in your seed all the families of the earth shall be blessed." Genesis 28:13-14 (NKJV)*

*"Then Jacob awoke from his sleep and said, "Surely the Lord is in this place, and I did not know it." Genesis 28:16 (NKJV)*

*"And he was afraid and said, "How awesome is this place! This is none other than the house of God, and this is the gate of heaven!*

*Then Jacob rose early in the morning and took the stone that he had put at his head, set it up as a pillar, and poured oil on top of it. And he called the name of that place Bethel; but the name of that city had been Luz previously." Genesis 28:17-19 (NKJV)*

This was Jacob's marker moment. What's yours?

_____

_____

_____

_____

_____

**Know this, your greatest insights into who God is, will come in your darkest moments.**

*"I, John, both your brother and companion in the tribulation and kingdom and patience of Jesus Christ, was on the island that is called Patmos for the word of God and for the testimony of Jesus Christ. I was in the Spirit on the Lord's Day, and I heard behind me a loud voice, as of a trumpet, saying, "I am the Alpha and the Omega, the First and the Last," and, "What you see, write in a book and send it to the seven churches which are in Asia: to Ephesus, to Smyrna, to Pergamos, to Thyatira, to Sardis, to Philadelphia, and to Laodicea." Revelation 1:9-11 (NKJV)*

---

**We judge the circumstances of our life from our limited perspective inside of those circumstances.**

---

*"But God, who is rich in mercy, because of His great love with which He loved us, even when we were dead in trespasses, made us alive together with Christ (by grace you have been saved), and raised us up together, and made us*

*sit together in the heavenly places in Christ Jesus, that in the ages to come He might show the exceeding riches of His grace in His kindness toward us in Christ Jesus." Ephesians 2:4-7 (NKJV)*

> **A change of perspective may not change your circum-stance, but it sure changes how you view it.**

# 1. The enemy's fiery darts can't pierce you.

They can't pierce you because your emotions are safely out of his reach. Did you know that his fiery darts have a limited range? When we're viewing things from the Father's perspective, the devil can't make it personal and use our emotions as pawns to keep us from the real issues. We see things the way they really are, which brings us to the next benefit.

## 2. You see things the way they really are from God's perspective.

I know we touched on this before, and yet it bears repeating. As we go through life, the way we view people and circumstances becomes distorted by hurts, disappointments, and experiences, and we begin to see life through clouded lenses. This happens to all of us on one level or another. Our only really safe bet is to see things from God's perspective. His view is always perfect because His lenses are never clouded. God has 20/20 spiritual vision.

## 3. You see beyond the circumstances to your answer.

> **Seeing our circumstance from God's perspective is seeing through the eyes of faith.**

*"Finally, brethren, whatever things are true, whatever things are noble, whatever things are just, whatever things are pure, whatever things are*

*lovely, whatever things are of good report, if there is any virtue and if there is anything praiseworthy—meditate on these things." Philippians 4:8 (NKJV)*

# 4. Your thinking becomes renewed.

*"And do not be conformed to this world, but be transformed by the renewing of your mind, that you may prove what is that good and acceptable and perfect will of God." Romans 12:2 (NKJV)*

*Then the Lord turned to him and said, "Go in this might of yours, and you shall save Israel from the hand of the Midianites. Have I not sent you?"*

*So he said to Him, "O my Lord, how can I save Israel? Indeed my clan is the weakest in Manasseh, and I am the least in my father's house." Judges 6:14-15 (NKJV)*

*"Then his companion answered and said, "This is nothing else but the sword of Gideon the son of Joash, a man of Israel! Into his hand God has delivered*

*Midian and the whole camp."* Gideon
*7:14 (NKJV)*

## 5. Your joy will increase.

LIFE IS
MEASURED
BY
MOMENTS

# Marker Moment

In this chapter, we saw that
because of our various experiences we all see life
through distorted lenses. We discovered this gives
us a slanted perspective on life and saw the
importance of gaining God's perspective through
right thinking. We were equipped with techniques
to help us clear the clouded lenses that skew our
perspective, so we can experience more of God's
joy in our lives.

1. Did you recognize any of the red flags of wrong
   thinking in your own life? Which one(s)?

   _____

   _____

   _____

   _____

What things can you do to correct them?

_____

_____

_____

_____

_____

2. One of the best ways to keep or gain joy and a correct perspective is by staying grateful. List three things you're grateful for. I recommend you start every morning with this exercise. Keep a gratitude journal, it's a great perspective adjuster. When you're having a rough day and everything seems negative, you can look back on the good and positive things that are in fact real in your life. This helps dispel the lie that everything is wrong. Take a few minutes to record some things you are grateful for here.

_____

_____

_____

_____

**Set a reminder** on your phone or calendar  so you won't forget to look back in a month or two at the huge difference this change has made in your quality of life, your mental attitude, and in your joy level.

# Prayer of Commitment

Father, help me to see my circumstances through Your lens, not mine. Remind me when I get down off my heavenly seat and begin to wallow in negativity to get back up where I belong. Help me to catch those negative thoughts that want to take up residence in my mind, and remind me of all the good things that are in my life. Help me to always honor You in thought, word, and deed. In Jesus' Name. Amen.

## Look Back

How has implementing these principles changed your attitude and perspective? Has anyone noticed the change in you? Who?

_____

_____

_____

_____

_____

What will you continue to work on?

_____

_____

_____

_____

_____

# SECTION 2

# THE HIDDEN BENEFITS OF OVERWHELMED

# Chapter 5

# The Gift of Too Much—Hand Something Off

## Connect with His Word

Exodus 18, Numbers 11

## One Minute Devotional

 Almost any leadership seminar you attend will talk about the art of delegation. Sometimes, we get overwhelmed, not because we're doing something wrong per se, but because we're missing this invaluable leadership principle. The story of Moses contains a great example of being overwhelmed because he was trying to do everything himself. If you're guilty of this, today's reading gives you a great opportunity to learn from someone else how to lose the burden of being overwhelmed. God never designed us to carry of it all ourselves.

> **There are times in your life that you're overwhelmed, not because you did something wrong, but because you did something right.**

*"I am not able to bear all these people alone, because the burden is too heavy for me." Numbers 11:14 (NKJV)*

> **No matter what's going on, God is never wrong.**

*So the Lord said to Moses: "Gather to Me seventy men of the elders of Israel, whom you know to be the elders of the people and officers over them; bring them to the tabernacle of meeting, that they may stand there with you. Then I will come down and talk with you there. I will take of the Spirit that is upon you and will put the same upon them; and they shall bear the burden of the people with you, that you may not bear it yourself alone." Numbers 11:16-17 (NKJV)*

Moses needed an army of helpers to help him manage his huge congregation. It was virtually an impossible task for him to do it alone.

> **God will allow you to stay in that overwhelmed state to teach you that you can't do it alone.**

> **The goal of leadership is reproduction.**

*"Train up a child in the way he should go,"* Proverbs 22:6a (NKJV)

> **The truth is this, we should be more shocked when we succeed than when we fail.**

> **We are earthen vessels with a hidden treasure called Jesus.**

*"Carry each other's burdens, and in this way you will fulfill the law of Christ."* Galatians 6:2 (NIV)

**What is the law of Christ? Love God, and love people.**

**It's my job to train and empower others.**

Who do I need to train?

_____

_____

_____

_____

_____

_____

*"After that generation died, another generation grew up who did not acknowledge the Lord or remember the mighty things he had done for Israel."* Judges 2:10 (NLT)

> **God created us to need one another. When we do everything ourselves, we are actually robbing someone else from using their God-given gift.**

What untapped potential do you see in that person? How can you help them use it?

_____

_____

_____

_____

_____

_____

LIFE IS
MEASURED
BY
MOMENTS

# Marker Moment

In this chapter, we learned from the life of Moses that at times God gives you the gift of overwhelmed, so you can learn to hand off things to others that are keeping you from God's best or are denying others from the opportunity to use their gifts.

1. Are you carrying burdens that are too heavy? Are there things you need to hand off? This could be at home, at work, or in any part of your life. List them here.

_____

_____

_____

_____

_____

_____

MONTH _____          YEAR _____

2. When will you commit to do that? On (date): _____.

Who will you delegate these things to?

_____

_____

_____

_____

_____

Do you need to train them? How will you do that?

_____

_____

_____

_____

_____

**Set a reminder** on your phone or calendar  for three-months for now to look back on the changes this has made.

## Prayer of Commitment

Father help me to search my heart and life to see the things that I am carrying that I need to hand off to someone else. Show me who that is and how I can come alongside of them to train them, encourage them, and lift them up. Thank You for teaching me Your system of multiplication and for using me to grow Your Kingdom. In Jesus' Name. Amen.

## Look Back

Now that you've handed these things off, and trained who you handed them off to, take a few minutes to reflect on how this has changed your world. Are you less stressed? List below how it's changed things for you. Has this caused you to grow and make more room for you to use your gifts? Has this allowed anyone else to use their gifts because you handed it off to them? If so, who? How have you seen them grow?

_____

_____

_____

_____

_____

_____

_____

_____

_____

_____

_____

What will you continue to work on?

_____

_____

_____

_____

_____

_____

# Chapter 6

# The Gift of Too Much—Put Something Down

## Connect with His Word

Luke 10

## One Minute Devotional

 Today's reading will also help you gain a deeper understanding of the last lesson, as well as this one. The chapter opens with Jesus delegating the spreading of the Good News to 72 of His disciples. Then, we have Martha. She put her tasks before relationship and not just any relationship, it was relationship with Jesus! Have you ever been guilty of that? I know I have. This is a pitfall that more task-oriented personalities are more prone to fall into, although any of us can be guilty of this trap. God wants to open your eyes to the things that really matter and remove the false guilt you feel when you feel the pressure of doing all that stuff you feel compelled to do. This week, I encourage you to take time to sit at His feet.

## Misplaced Priorities

*"But Martha was distracted by all the preparations that had to be made. She came to him and asked, "Lord, don't you care that my sister has left me to do the work by myself? Tell her to help me!"?" Luke 10:40 (NIV)*

Do you find at times you get your priorities mixed up? Jot down a time that happened and the results.

_____

_____

_____

_____

_____

*"Going a little farther, he fell with his face to the ground and prayed, "My Father, if it is possible, may this cup be taken from me. Yet not as I will, but as you will." Matthew 26:39 (NIV)*

> **The reason many of us have a disappointing prayer life is we pray directive prayers versus direct prayers.**

Have you ever been guilty of telling God what He should give you, or how He should do His job?

_____

_____

_____

_____

_____

How did that go for you?

_____

_____

_____

_____

_____

*"And Jesus answered and said to her, "Martha, Martha, you are worried and troubled about many things. But one thing is needed, and Mary has chosen that good part, which will not be taken away from her." Luke 10:41-42 (NKJV)*

*"But the Lord God called to the man, "Where are you?" Genesis 3:9 (NIV)*

**Stress is a symptom, not the root problem.**

**In letting go, you make room to receive from God the thing that truly matters most.**

*"for God's gifts and his call are irrevocable." Romans 11:29 (NIV)*

*"I know where I came from and where I am going." John 8:14b (NLT)*

*"Turn my eyes from worthless things; preserve my life according to your word." Psalms 119:37 (NIV)*

> **You will never live an enriched life filling it with worthless things.**

**LIFE IS MEASURED BY MOMENTS**

# Marker Moment

In this chapter, we saw from the life of Martha, that she needed to put some things down. Even though she was well meaning, she had her priorities wrong. We also learned that stress is a symptom and not the root problem, and that sometimes our prayer life looks more like a honey-do List than fellowship with the God of the universe. If we're not careful, we can start telling God what to do instead of praying the prayers of a willing heart.

1. Are there things in your life you need to put down? What are they?

_____

_____

_____

_____

_____

MONTH _____        YEAR _____

Date(s) you put them down: _____.

2. How can you reprioritize your calendar? What did you change?

_____

_____

_____

_____

_____

_____

**Set a reminder** on your phone or calendar for 30 days so you can look back at how these changes impacted your life and family. Then make sure you look back occasionally to make sure you're staying on track and old habits are not creeping back in.

## Prayer of Commitment

Father, I ask You that You show me the areas of my life that I'm being a Martha instead of a Mary. Help me to set my priorities with an eternal  mindset. I thank You for Your help with this. In Jesus' Name. Amen.

## Look Back

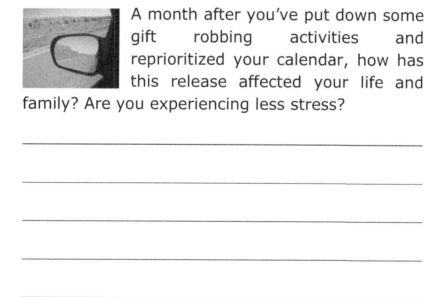 A month after you've put down some gift robbing activities and reprioritized your calendar, how has this release affected your life and family? Are you experiencing less stress?

_____

_____

_____

_____

_____

_____

What will you continue to work on?

_____

_____

_____

_____

_____

_____

# Chapter 7

# The Gift of Too Much—Hand Something Off to God

## Connect with His Word

2 Corinthians 11:23-12:10,
Philippians 4:8

## One Minute Devotional

Remember the old song, *I Never Promised You a Rose Garden*? Well, God never promised us a rose garden either. This is clearly demonstrated in the life of Paul. The key we see from our reading is what you focus on in those times of trial makes all the difference. There are times when you just need to give it to the Lord because it is way too big for you to handle. This is not only our smartest move because it keeps us humble, but it also gives God the space to do what only He can do. Philippians 4:8 contains an important truth to help us keep our focus right, it's about what you think about, not just a glancing thought but what you allow your mind to dwell on. Are you spinning your wheels dwelling on what's happening in the natural? Or, are you thinking what the word teaches us to do, that is to have thoughts of the good, the positive, and the God glorifying?

_____

_____

_____

_____

_____

*"Even if I should choose to boast, I would not be a fool, because I would be speaking the truth. But I refrain, so no one will think more of me than is warranted by what I do or say, or because of these surpassingly great revelations. Therefore, in order to keep me from becoming conceited, I was given a thorn in my flesh, a messenger of Satan, to torment me. Three times I pleaded with the Lord to take it away from me." 2 Corinthians 12:6-8 (NIV)*

*"But he said to me, "My grace is sufficient for you, for my power is made perfect in weakness." 2 Corinthians 12:9a (NIV)*

*"Therefore I will boast all the more gladly about my weaknesses, so that Christ's power may rest on me. That is why, for Christ's sake, I delight in weaknesses, in insults, in hardships, in persecutions, in difficulties. For when I am weak, then I am strong."* 2 Corinthians 12:9b-10 (NIV)

**The gift of too much teaches us to hand something off to God.**

**Feelings aren't facts; they're just feelings.**

Be honest with yourself, do you ever treat your feelings as though they were facts? What was the fruit of that? In other words, how did that go for you?

_____

_____

_____

_____

*"God made him who had no sin to be sin for us, so that in him we might become the righteousness of God." 2 Corinthians 5:21 (NIV)*

> **When we come to the end of ourselves, it's the beginning of God.**

*"And lest I should be exalted above measure by the abundance of the revelations, a thorn in the flesh was given to me, a messenger of Satan to buffet me, lest I be exalted above measure." 2 Corinthians 12:7 (NKJV)*

> **There is a difference between God allowing and God causing something.**

Another honesty moment. Have you ever blamed God for something that happened to you, or for a poor choice you actually made yourself? When was a time you did that? In retrospect, how would you handle that differently if it happened today?

_____

_____

_____

_____

_____

_____

*"I have worked much harder, been in prison more frequently, been flogged more severely, and been exposed to death again and again. Five times I received from the Jews the forty lashes minus one. Three times I was beaten with rods, once I was pelted with stones, three times I was shipwrecked, I spent a night and a day in the open sea, I have been constantly on the move. I have been in danger from rivers, in danger from bandits, in danger from my fellow Jews, in danger from Gentiles; in danger in the city, in*

*danger in the country, in danger at sea; and in danger from false believers. I have labored and toiled and have often gone without sleep; I have known hunger and thirst and have often gone without food; I have been cold and naked. Besides everything else, I face daily the pressure of my concern for all the churches. Who is weak, and I do not feel weak? Who is led into sin, and I do not inwardly burn?*

*If I must boast, I will boast of the things that show my weakness. The God and Father of the Lord Jesus, who is to be praised forever, knows that I am not lying. In Damascus the governor under King Aretas had the city of the Damascenes guarded in order to arrest me. But I was lowered in a basket from a window in the wall and slipped through his hands." 2 Corinthians 11:23b-33 (NIV)*

*"Therefore most gladly I will rather boast in my infirmities, that the power of Christ may rest upon me." 2 Corinthians 12:9b (NKJV)*

> **There is a difference between a thorn in the flesh and carrying a cross for Christ.**

"If any of you wants to be my follower, you must give up your own way, take up your cross, and follow me." Matthew 16b:24 (NLT)

# 1. Every limitation is an opportunity for an illumination.

"Then some Jews came from Antioch and Iconium and won the crowd over. They stoned Paul and dragged him outside the city, thinking he was dead. But after the disciples had gathered around him, he got up and went back into the city. The next day he and Barnabas left for Derbe." Acts 14:19-20 (NIV)

## 2. Weakness is not a limitation, but an invitation.

> **I will never have a big God as long as I have a big me.**

Have you suffered under the misconception that you show God as strong by muscling through a crisis in your own strength? What was the result of that?

_____

_____

_____

_____

_____

_____

_____

## 3. God uses what we want changed to change us.

Reflect on a time when you asked God to change something in your life and He did not change it, but you ended up better on the other side?

_____

_____

_____

_____

_____

LIFE IS MEASURED BY MOMENTS

## Marker Moment

In this chapter, we learned that there are times when we just need to hand something off to God. This chapter also pulled the curtain back on some misconceptions that we might hold in regard to how God works, and we learned the difference between a thorn and a cross.

1.  Do you have something you need to hand off
to God? What is it?

_____

_____

_____

_____

_____

2.  Do you have things you're trying to carry in
your own strength? What will you do to hand them
off to God?

_____

_____

_____

_____

_____

**Set a reminder** on your phone or calendar
to look back in 30 to 60 days to reflect on
how much less stressed you are.

## Prayer of Commitment

Father, I ask that You show me the things in my life that I am trying to carry that I need to just give to You. Please help me to embrace the changes that You want to make in me. I ask You to help me get out of the way so You can be the big God in my life that You truly are. With all my heart, I want Your highest and best for my life. In Jesus' Name. Amen.

## Look Back

Now that a month or two have passed, and you're no longer carrying weights you were never meant to carry, what has changed?

_____

_____

_____

_____

_____

What will you continue to work on?

_____

_____

_____

_____

_____

_____

# SECTION 3

# WHY WE GET OVERWHELMED AND HOW TO ESCAPE

# Chapter 8

# The Outside Factor:

# Sin, Satan, and the Fall

## Connect with His Word

Psalm 21, Jeremiah 29:11-13

## One Minute Devotional

 The Lord wants to walk with you through all your valleys and mountain tops. Satan's scheme is to get you to believe you can't trust the One who wants to be with you every step of the way. His goal for your life is to shipwreck your faith. One of our jobs as a believer is to stand in faith. When everything around us seems like it is falling apart, we are to keep standing in faith. When we don't see an answer, keep standing. Hebrews 11:1 tells us faith is trusting in God when we don't see the answer. It takes no faith to believe when we can see the answer. Often when you're going through a valley, do you ever run so fast in your own strength trying to get out of the valley, that you leave God back there in the dust. God wants to walk with you through the valley, just like He wants you to walk with Him on the mountain tops.

> *"Then God said, 'Let Us make man in Our image, according to Our likeness; let them have dominion over the fish of the sea, over the birds of the air, and over the cattle, over all the earth and over every creeping thing that creeps on the earth.'" Genesis 1:26 (NKJV)*

> *"Then the Lord God took the man and put him in the garden of Eden to tend and keep it. And the Lord God commanded the man, saying, "Of every tree of the garden you may freely eat; but of the tree of the knowledge of good and evil you shall not eat, for in the day that you eat of it you shall surely die." Genesis 2:15-17 (NKJV)*

**Satan has, and always will, question God's character.**

Have you been guilty of the same sin as Adam and Eve? I think we all have. When was a time you questioned God's character?

_____

_____

_____

_____

_____

_____

*"And I saw in the right hand of Him who sat on the throne a scroll written inside and on the back, sealed with seven seals. Then I saw a strong angel proclaiming with a loud voice, "Who is worthy to open the scroll and to loose its seals?" And no one in heaven or on the earth or under the earth was able to open the scroll, or to look at it.*

*So I wept much, because no one was found worthy to open and read the scroll, or to look at it." Revelation 5:1-4 (NKJV)*

*"But one of the elders said to me, "Do not weep. Behold, the Lion of the tribe of Judah, the Root of David, has prevailed to open the scroll and to loose its seven seals." Revelation 5:5 (NKJV)*

*"Satan, who is the god of this world, has blinded the minds of those who don't believe. They are unable to see the glorious light of the Good News. They don't understand this message about the glory of Christ, who is the exact likeness of God."* 2 Corinthians 4:4 (NLT)

Who has God brought into your life who doesn't know Jesus? Will you pray for them? Will you tell them what God has done in your life?

_____

_____

_____

_____

MONTH _____     YEAR _____

Date I shared with my friend:

_____.

LIFE IS MEASURED BY MOMENTS

## Marker Moment

In this chapter, we pulled back the curtain on Satan's bag of tricks and we saw how sin entered the world through man's choice to disobey God. His goal is to discredit God's character, and in the process get us to doubt His goodness. When he succeeds, he has successfully undermined our ability to trust God and he has defused our faith.

1. Are there areas where you struggle with Satan's Panther Martin lure, so you can't trust God? What areas are they?

_____

_____

_____

_____

_____

_____

2. In the future, how can you guard your heart against this lie?

_____

_____

_____

_____

_____

_____

**Set a reminder** on your phone or calendar this time. Let's reel it in to two weeks for a look back.

# Prayer of Commitment

Father show me any area where I am believing the lies of Satan in my life. I ask Your forgiveness for ever questioning Your motives,  character, or goodness. Thank You for forgiving me. In Jesus' Name. Amen.

## Look Back

In just this short time, has implementing these changes made a difference in how you view God? How has this realization helped your walk with God? Don't forget to look back again in the near future.

_____

_____

_____

_____

_____

What will you continue to work on?

_____

_____

_____

_____

_____

# Chapter 9

# So, What's That to Me?

## Connect with His Word

1 Peter 2, Isaiah 14:12-21

## One Minute Devotional

 Have you ever been guilty of giving Satan way more credit than he deserves? I know I have. Or, how about this? Have you given him credit for things that were just your flesh getting its own way? Sometimes we can give Satan way more focus and credit than he really deserves. After all he is a defeated foe. Jesus took care of him at the cross.

Now, it's your job to keep your focus on Jesus, the author and finisher of your faith. When you're focusing on Jesus, you'll have much more joy and peace in the journey—and many more victories. Decide today to stop allowing the enemy to have any more power in your life. Then, choose to believe what God's word says instead of what your experience or other voices in your life are telling you. You will be amazed at the change this makes in your life.

> **Satan only has as much power as you allow him to have.**

What areas have you given Satan power in your life? It could be a habit, an attitude, a belief about yourself or others, that is unbiblical.

_____

_____

_____

_____

_____

_____

*"My people are destroyed for lack of knowledge."* Hosea 4:6a (NKJV)

# 1. Acknowledge I have a filter.

> **Every human being has filters.**

What are your filters? If you're not sure, ask a good friend or loved one for their insight.

_____

_____

_____

_____

_____

_____

> **Don't build theology on your experience, you build theology on the Bible.**

Is there a belief you hold that is simply built on your experience or that of someone you know, and not on what God's Word says? What is that false belief?

_____

_____

_____

_____

_____

| **Let God interpret life for you versus allowing life to interpret God for you.** |
| --- |

# 2. Acknowledge I'm not always right.

| **God is inexhaustible.** |
| --- |

*"For now we see in a mirror, dimly, but then face to face. Now I know in part, but then I shall know just as I also am known." 1 Corinthians 13:12 (NKJV)*

Have you ever been guilty of an "I already know all that," attitude? If so, what brought you out of it? Or...are you still there?

_____

_____

_____

_____

_____

_____

## 3. Acknowledge what I believe doesn't change the truth.

> **My goal is not to impress you, my goal is to impact you.**

## 4. What I believe impacts my life.

*"Then you will know the truth, and the truth will set you free." John 8:32 (NIV)*

Are there things you've believed that have either had a negative or positive impact on your life? What are they?

_____

_____

_____

_____

_____

> **If truth sets us free, then a lie believed to be true can make us bound.**

Are there any lies you've believed that are holding you back? What are they, and how are they holding you back?

_____

_____

_____

_____

> **All behavior is a by-product of what we believe.**

Do you have any behaviors that expose a lie you believed? If so, what are they and why do you think you believed them?

_____

_____

_____

_____

_____

_____

*"What must we do to do the works God requires?" John 6:28b (NIV)*

*"The work of God is this: to believe in the one he has sent." John 6:29b (NIV)*

> **The work that you and I have isn't to change our behavior, it is to change our belief.**

LIFE IS MEASURED BY MOMENTS

## Marker Moment

In this chapter, it was discovered that you have filters that skew how you see your world. Everyone does. These filters affect what you believe and what you believe effects the entire direction of your life. We also saw that all behavior is a product of what you believe.

1. Being honest with yourself, are there things you've believed to be true, but aren't true? What are they?

_____

_____

_____

_____

_____

_____

_____

2. Using the filter of God's Word, how can you adjust your thinking?

_____

_____

_____

_____

_____

_____

**Set a reminder** on your phone or calendar for 30 to 60 days, so you can look back and see how your thinking has cleared up. Then don't forget to keep looking back.

## Prayer of Commitment

Father, search my heart and show me if there are lies I've believed, but am not aware of. Please bring these to the light and make the truth clear to me  so I can correct my beliefs. In Jesus' Name. Amen.

# Look Back

 Your reminder has alerted you that it is time to look back. Now that you've implemented these changes, look back over this page and reflect on the changes you have seen. Be sure to take time to express your gratitude to God. He has set you free from some of your wrong thinking!

_____

_____

_____

_____

What will you continue to work on?

_____

_____

_____

_____

_____

# Chapter 10

# The Enemy Factor—The Backstory

## Connect with His Word

Proverbs 3

## One Minute Devotional

 When you read Proverbs 3, you'll notice that it contains many statements that say, if you do this, then God will do that. The Word of God is filled with many "if-then's." They are God telling us, "If you do this, then I'll do that." God always has our best interest at heart. When we follow His ways, we live the blessed life, not a trouble-free life. A blessed life is one of hope, joy, and peace no matter what we are going through at the moment. This is one of the best ways to break any strongholds Satan may have in your mind. When we're walking in the will of God, you have an invisible shield of protection around you. Being in God's will is always the safest place to be. So, when God tells you, "If you do this, I'll do that," don't hesitate. Just do it! Let Him show Himself strong on your behalf.

> **Satan is happy to let you get in a ditch, because he knows you are going nowhere.**

Would Satan consider you a threat to his plans? Why or why not?

_____

_____

_____

_____

_____

_____

"And without faith it is impossible to please God," Hebrews 11:6a (NIV)

"Through faith and patience, we inherit the promises." Hebrews 11:12 (NKJV)

"Then the Lord God called to Adam and said to him, 'Where are you?'" Genesis 3:9 (NKJV)

> **A lot of people avoid God because they don't want to have to come to terms with where they are.**

Do you ever find yourself attempting to hide from God? What is it you think you are hiding from? Why don't you want to come to terms with where you are?

_____

_____

_____

_____

_____

_____

*"So Satan answered the Lord and said, "From going to and fro on the earth, and from walking back and forth on it." Job 1:7b (NKJV)*

*"Be sober, be vigilant; because your adversary the devil walks about like a roaring lion, seeking whom he may devour. Resist him, steadfast in the faith, knowing that the same sufferings*

*are experienced by your brotherhood in the world." 1 Peter 5:8-9 (NKJV)*

Are you convinced that Satan is a real spiritual being, or do you believe he is just a metaphor for evil? Why do you believe this?

_____

_____

_____

_____

_____

_____

**We don't fight for victory; we fight from victory.**

*"In this way, he disarmed the spiritual rulers and authorities. He shamed them publicly by his victory over them on the cross." Colossians 2:15 (NLT)*

*"For He shall give His angels charge over you,*
*To keep you in all your ways." Psalm 91:11 (NKJV)*

*"The steps of a good man are ordered by the Lord, And He delights in his way."* Psalm 37:23 (NKJV)

*"Therefore submit to God. Resist the devil and he will flee from you."* James 4:7 (NKJV)

> **You can quote the Word, but if you're not submitted to it, it's like firing a gun without bullets.**

Is your spiritual gun loaded and ready to fire, or are you out of bullets? Why do you think that is?

_____

_____

_____

_____

*"But my God shall supply all your need according to his riches in glory by Christ Jesus."* Philippians 4:19 (King James Version)

> *"Bring all the tithes into the storehouse, That there may be food in My house, And try Me now in this," Says the Lord of hosts, "If I will not open for you the windows of heaven, And pour out for you such blessing, That there will not be room enough to receive it."*

> *"And I will rebuke the devourer for your sakes, So that he will not destroy the fruit of your ground, Nor shall the vine fail to bear fruit for you in the field," Says the Lord of hosts; Malachi 3:10-11 (NKJV)*

This is the only place in scripture where God says, go ahead and challenge Me. The word tithe means 1/10th or 10% and the storehouse He's referring to here would be the local church. So, question? Are you a tither? If not, I want to encourage you to take God's challenge, test Him and see if He means what He says. Give it 90 days.

I started my tithe challenge on _____ date.

"And the evil spirit answered and said,
"Jesus I know, and Paul I know; but
who are you?" Acts 19:15 (NKJV)

"Having disarmed principalities and
powers, He made a public spectacle of
them, triumphing over them in it."
Colossians 2:15 (NKJV)

"You are of God, little children, and
have overcome them, because He who
is in you is greater than he who is in the
world." 1 John 4:4 (NKJV)

> **When we worship, it's
> declaring that Jesus is our
> Lord.**

"I, Jesus, have sent My angel to testify
to you these things in the churches. I
am the Root and the Offspring of David,
the Bright and Morning Star."
Revelations 22:16 (NKJV)

"For the eyes of the Lord run to and fro
throughout the whole earth, to show
Himself strong on behalf of those whose
heart is loyal to Him." 2 Chronicles
16:9a (NKJV)

> **God's eyes are running to and fro looking for someone that He can empower.**

*"But beware of men, for they will deliver you up to councils and scourge you in their synagogues. You will be brought before governors and kings for My sake, as a testimony to them and to the Gentiles. But when they deliver you up, do not worry about how or what you should speak. For it will be given to you in that hour what you should speak; for it is not you who speak, but the Spirit of your Father who speaks in you."*
*Matthew 10:17-20 (NKJV)*

LIFE IS MEASURED BY MOMENTS

# Marker Moment

In this chapter, we learned that our enemy, Satan, is a real eternal being, not a metaphor, and Jesus defeated him at the cross. We also discovered there are two ditches that people tend to fall in, one that believes Satan is a metaphor for evil, and the other who believe Satan is responsible for every problem. When you're in a ditch, you're not going anywhere. Additionally, we learned how to resist Satan's attacks and how being submitted to the Word is the most effective weapon against the enemy.

1. Do you find yourself in one of those ditches? Which one?

_____

_____

_____

_____

_____

_____

2. If you're in the ditch, how will you get out?

_____

_____

_____

_____

_____

_____

How will you resist the devil in your own life, now that you know he has limited authority?

_____

_____

_____

_____

_____

**Set a reminder** on your phone or calendar for three months then go to the **Look Back** section for this chapter to reflect on how the changes you've made in your financial commitment to God and your thought life have changed your outward life.

# Prayer of Commitment

Father, I ask that You make me aware of the activity of the enemy in my life and ask that You help me to use Your Word to stand against his tactics. Thank You that he is a defeated foe. Help me to keep my focus on You the author and finisher of my faith and not Your defeated enemy. I will honor You with ten percent of my earnings and put my trust in

Your provision for me, not my paycheck. May my thoughts, the words of my mouth, and my actions bring glory and honor to Your name. In Jesus' Name. Amen.

## Look Back

 After applying the principles you gleaned from this chapter, how has it changed the way you view problems? How about your finances? Look over the last six months of your records. Are you more or less financially stable after honoring God with your 10% for the last three months than you were in the previous three months before tithing?

_____

_____

_____

_____

_____

What will you continue to work on?

_____

_____

_____

_____

_____

# Chapter 11

# The Enemy Factor—The Rest of the Story

## Connect with His Word

1 John 2, I Thessalonians 5:14-18

## One Minute Devotional

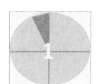
In 1 Thessalonians 5:14-18 (NLT) we find Paul giving us great advice on how to live the Christian life in general and he turns his focus particularly on how to get through life's struggles.

> "Brothers and sisters, we urge you to warn those who are lazy. Encourage those who are timid. Take tender care of those who are weak. Be patient with everyone.
>
> See that no one pays back evil for evil, but always try to do good to each other and to all people.

*Always be joyful. Never stop praying.*
*Be thankful in all circumstances, for this*
*is God's will for you who belong to*
*Christ Jesus." 1 Thessalonians 5:14-18*
*(NLT)*

He first gives us how as people or as Christians we are to treat others. Let me stop here for a minute. Remember when we attack others and speak ill of them, we're doing the enemy's work. How we treat others determines our witness to the world and to a large extent our personal peace. We can't treat others who God created with distain and expect our own life to be a bed of roses because we are in direct violation to God's word.

Next, he turns the focus onto you and me to equip us to overcome anything that comes our way. He gives us the dynamic trio: joy, prayer, and gratitude. Notice it doesn't say to be thankful when everything is going great, he says in all circumstances. Remember, He promises to make all things work for our good. We're not thankful for all things, we're thankful in all things. That's a totally different thing.

"Have you considered My servant *Job,*
*that there is none like him on the earth,*
*a blameless and upright man, one who*
*fears God and shuns evil?" Job 1:8b*
*(NKJV)*

> *"So Satan answered the Lord and said, "Does Job fear God for nothing? Have You not made a hedge around him, around his household, and around all that he has on every side? You have blessed the work of his hands, and his possessions have increased in the land." Job 1:9-10 (NKJV)*

> **God has our back when Satan is on the attack.**

What is your first reaction when you are under attack? Do you tend to blame God?

_____

_____

_____

_____

_____

> **Job's life is a picture of how we survive suffering and move to thriving on the other side.**

How do you view suffering in your life?

_____

_____

_____

_____

_____

_____

*Then I heard a loud voice saying in heaven, "Now salvation, and strength, and the kingdom of our God, and the power of His Christ have come, for the accuser of our brethren, who accused them before our God day and night, has been cast down. And they overcame him by the blood of the Lamb and by the word of their testimony, and they did not love their lives to the death." Revelation 12:10-11 (NKJV)*

> **God allows suffering, to silence Satan.**

> **Job's love for God silenced Satan.**

When the accuser throws accusations at you, do you believe them? Have you been guilty of leaving Jesus your advocate, and running over to the prosecutions side and agreeing with them? If so, how did that go?

_____

_____

_____

_____

_____

_____

*"And the Philistine said, "I defy the armies of Israel this day; give me a man, that we may fight together." 1 Samuel 17:10 (NKJV)*

*Then David said to the Philistine, "You come to me with a sword, with a spear, and with a javelin. But I come to you in the name of the Lord of hosts, the God of the armies of Israel, whom you have defied. This day the Lord will deliver you into my hand, and I will strike you and take your head from you. And this day I will give the carcasses of the camp of the Philistines to the birds of the air and the wild beasts of the earth, that all the earth may know that there is a God in Israel. Then all this assembly shall know that the Lord does not save with sword and spear; for the battle is the Lord's, and He will give you into our hands." 1 Samuel 17:45-47 (NKJV)*

---

**He has blessed you, so serve Him because of who He is, not because of His gifts.**

---

*"My dear children, I am writing this to you so that you will not sin. But if anyone does sin, we have an advocate who pleads our case before the Father. He is Jesus Christ, the one who is truly righteous." 1 John 2:1 (NLT)*

*"For He made Him who knew no sin to be sin for us, that we might become the righteousness of God in Him."* 2 Corinthian 5:21 (NKJV)

> **Our job is this, to agree with Jesus.**

Who have you been agreeing with?

_____

_____

_____

_____

_____

_____

> **I'm so glad that we serve a God who sees us as we can be and not as we are.**

LIFE IS
MEASURED
BY
MOMENTS

# Marker Moment

In this chapter, we saw that Job's life is a picture showing us how to survive suffering and come out on top on the other side. We discovered Jesus is our defense attorney in the court of Heaven and that Satan is the prosecutor who slings accusations regarding our failures and inadequacies at us. We came to the realization that often we side with the prosecution instead of our own defender and advocate Jesus. Perhaps our most painful revelation was that the church is the Bride of Christ and when we bash other churches and believers, we are actually doing the work of the accuser, Satan.

1. Is there an area in your life where you're experiencing suffering? Record it here.

_____

_____

_____

_____

_____

2. List several keys from this chapter you found encouraging.

_____

_____

_____

_____

_____

_____

3. Have you found yourself guilty of doing the devil's work at times by bashing other believers or churches? Going forward, how will you curtail this temptation?

_____

_____

_____

_____

_____

**Set a reminder** on your phone or calendar to **Look Back** when the current trial has passed to see how you're progressing with your attitude toward suffering, who you're agreeing with, and who you're advocating for.

## Look Back

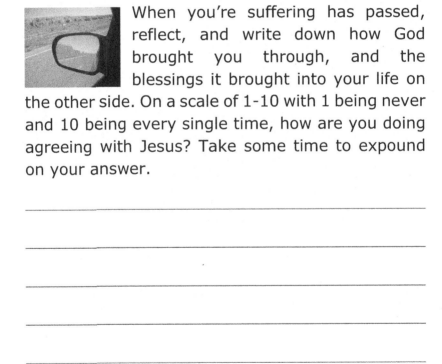 When you're suffering has passed, reflect, and write down how God brought you through, and the blessings it brought into your life on the other side. On a scale of 1-10 with 1 being never and 10 being every single time, how are you doing agreeing with Jesus? Take some time to expound on your answer.

_____

_____

_____

_____

_____

_____

What will you continue to work on?

_____

_____

_____

_____

_____

_____

# Chapter 12

# Pain Has Purpose

*Help! I've Fallen and I Need Help Getting Up*

## Connect with His Word

Matthew 26:69-75, Acts 2

## One Minute Devotional

 Are you like me when you read about Peter's denial of Jesus? Do you think, "Would I have done the same thing as Peter?" Can you imagine how he must have felt when that rooster crowed? If it was me, I'd think, "Well, God is done with me this time for sure." However, that was not the case. God was far from done with Peter. He still had big, and I mean big, plans for his life. This should encourage us, because the truth is, we've all been a Peter at one time or another. Skip to the book of Acts and the Holy Spirit comes—and guess who is there with the other disciples to receive the gift of the Spirit? That's right, Peter. Then, he goes out and boldly preaches and 3,000 people give their lives to Christ.

No matter who you are or what you've done, God is not done with you. If you're still drawing breath, He has a plan for your life. Just say, "Here I am Lord, use me."

> *"The thief does not come except to steal, and to kill, and to destroy. I have come that they may have life, and that they may have it more abundantly."*
> *John 10:10 (NKJV)*

**You can fall, but if you get back up, that's not failing, it is falling forward.**

What's your reaction when you fail?

_____

_____

_____

_____

_____

_____

*"For a righteous man may fall seven times And rise again," Proverbs 24:16a (NKJV)*

> **God wants to make your greatest mess, into your greatest message.**

# Number 1: Pride. Pride is the beginning of a fall.

*"Pride goes before destruction, a haughty spirit before a fall." Proverbs 16:18 (NIV)*

*"God resists the proud, But gives grace to the humble." James 4:6b (NKJV)*

On one level or another, we all deal with pride. How is your pride expressed?

_____

_____

_____

_____

## Number 2: Follow Jesus at a distance.

Is there any area of your life that you're following Jesus at a distance? What is it?

_____

_____

_____

_____

_____

## Number 3: Go to the world for comfort.

Do you ever go the world for comfort? How?

_____

_____

_____

_____

_____

> **The good news is this: even if you find yourself flat on your face, know this, Jesus isn't done with you.**

> **Would anyone want to be a Christian after following your social media posts?**

What about your social media posts? Would they make someone want to be a Christian after reading them? Why do you think this?

_____

_____

_____

_____

_____

_____

*"No temptation has overtaken you except such as is common to man; but God is faithful, who will not allow you to be tempted beyond what you are able, but with the temptation will also make*

*the way of escape, that you may be able to bear it." 1 Corinthians 10:13 (NKJV)*

**One of the biggest lies of the enemy is this, "You're the only one."**

Have you ever felt like you were the only one who had ever gone through what you were going through? What do you think made you feel that way?

_____

_____

_____

_____

_____

_____

_____

Think back to a time when you were going through a really hard time. Did you feel like no one could understand? Why did you think that?

_____

_____

_____

_____

_____

_____

When you came out of the hard time, did you still feel the same? Why?

_____

_____

_____

_____

_____

_____

In your life with Christ, when you encounter "emergencies," notice that there's always an exit.

There's always a space between suffering and the solution.

"And the Lord restored Job's losses when he prayed for his friends. Indeed the Lord gave Job twice as much as he had before. Now the Lord blessed the latter days of Job more than his beginning; for he had fourteen thousand sheep, six thousand camels, one thousand yoke of oxen, and one thousand female donkeys. He also had seven sons and three daughters." Job 42:10 & 12-13 (NKJV)

When God does not stop a trial, He will use it for the good. Think of a hard time you've gone through. What was the good that came out of that trial in the end?

_____

_____

_____

_____

_____

**When we get to heaven, you will never find anyone walking around saying, "Is this all there is?"**

*"Indeed, we count them blessed who endure. You have heard of the perseverance of Job and seen the end intended by the Lord—that the Lord is very compassionate and merciful." James 5:11 (NKJV)*

> **When you feel it's the end, and you haven't yet seen God's intent; don't quit.**

> **Remember, He writes the last chapter and it's always better than the first.**

LIFE IS MEASURED BY MOMENTS

# Marker Moment

In this chapter, we learned from the life of Peter what not to do when you're facing failure or fear of failure. We also learned from Job to persevere, because God has something good for you on the other side of suffering if you don't quit.

1. Have you found yourself ever taking one or more of the steps just to fall flat on your face? List them.

_____

_____

_____

_____

2.   What steps do you need to take to get back on track?

_____

_____

_____

_____

_____

_____

3.   How has this chapter impacted your view of failure?

_____

_____

_____

_____

_____

_____

4.   Are there areas in your life where you have been tempted to quit? What are they? Has this chapter changed your perspective on suffering?

_____

_____

_____

_____

**Set a reminder** on your phone or calendar to **Look Back.** Change always occurs incrementally so it is often hard to see. When we stop and look back, we can see how far we've come. So, I encourage you, don't forget to **Look Back** or you may miss the blessing of what God is or has done in your life.

## Prayer of Commitment

Father, let me set my face like a flint to keep going in the face of my trials knowing You have something good for me at the other end. Please convict me and show me if I get into pride, or begin to drift, or go to the world for comfort. Let me always represent You well. In Jesus' Name. Amen.

# Look Back

After you've taken these steps, what differences do you see in your life?

_____

_____

_____

_____

_____

_____

What will you continue to work on?

_____

_____

_____

_____

_____

# Chapter 13

# How to Get Out of Overwhelm

## Connect with His Word

Matthew 14:22-33, Matthew
16:19, Isaiah 22:22, Revelation 3:7, Luke 11:52

## One Minute Devotional

As I was pondering this chapter, it struck me that it contained four keys for getting out of overwhelmed. A key is something that opens or closes locks—literally or metaphorically. The term key is only used in Scripture six times. It is used metaphorically in Matthew 16:19 and Luke 11:52. It is used as a symbol of power and authority in Isaiah 22:22 and Revelation 3:7.

This is exciting news for you and me. As you look into the Word of God, He gives you the keys that open your understanding to His truth that will set you free. But remember, there is a difference between having a key and using a key. Use the keys God is giving you to unlock whatever is holding you back from the best version of yourself. Sometimes it takes courage to open a new door, because you don't know what you will find on the other side. Remember, Jesus came to give you life abundantly. Like Peter, you'll never walk on water until you step out of the boat. Go ahead, use the keys!

# Key 1: Realize It.

> *"And Peter answered Him and said, "Lord, if it is You, command me to come to You on the water." So, He said, "Come." And when Peter had come down out of the boat, he walked on the water to go to Jesus." Matthew 14:28-29 (NKJV)*

> **To walk on the water, Peter first had to get out of the boat.**

Are you sitting in that proverbial boat? What fear do you need to walk on?

_____

_____

_____

_____

_____

_____

When you keep your eyes on Jesus, you won't sink.

> *"And when they got into the boat, the wind ceased." Matthew 14:32 (NKJV)*

Do you see your problems as opportunities? Why or why not?

_____

_____

_____

_____

_____

## Key 2: Release It.

> **Faith changes things. Prayer changes us.**

*"But the boat was now in the middle of the sea, tossed by the waves, for the wind was contrary." Matthew 14:24 (NKJV)*

*"Now in the fourth watch of the night Jesus went to them, walking on the sea. And when the disciples saw Him walking on the sea," Matthew 14: 25-26a (NKJV)*

> **If all our problems instantly evaporated, it would take neither faith nor trust.**

## Key 3: Replace It.

*"Death and life are in the power of the tongue, and those who love it will eat its fruit." Proverbs 18:21 (NKJV)*

> **Our faith should be in God, not in our problem.**

Is your faith in your God or in your problem? Are you speaking about your problem or to your problem? What is the evidence that makes you think this?

_____

_____

_____

_____

_____

_____

*"So then faith comes by hearing, and hearing by the word of God." Romans 10:17 (NKJV)*

*"For assuredly, I say to you, whoever says to this mountain, 'Be removed and be cast into the sea,' and does not doubt in his heart, but believes that those things he says will be done, he will have whatever he says. Therefore I say to you, whatever things you ask*

*when you pray, believe that you receive them, and you will have them." Mark 11:23 -24 (NKJV)*

> **We resist the enemy, and we resist our problems with the authority of God's Word; that's our sword.**

Do you spend time in God's Word every day? How can you improve in this habit?

_____

_____

_____

_____

_____

_____

# Key 4: Request It.

*"Be anxious for nothing, but in everything by prayer and supplication, with thanksgiving, let your requests be*

*made known to God;" Philippians 4:6 (NKJV)*

*"But when he saw that the wind was boisterous, he was afraid; and beginning to sink he cried out, saying, "Lord, save me!" And immediately Jesus stretched out His hand and caught him," Matthew 14:30-31a (NKJV)*

**When we take our eyes off Jesus and onto our problem, we will always begin to sink.**

On a scale from 1 to 10 with 1 being non-existent and 10 being I spend most of my day praying, how would you rate your prayer life? _____

What could you do to bring that number up?

_____

_____

_____

_____

_____

LIFE IS MEASURED BY MOMENTS

# Marker Moment

In this chapter, we explored four keys that give you the necessary steps you need to take to get out of overwhelmed. First, we saw that you need to realize overwhelmed is not the root issue, it's lack of vision. Second, you need to release it to God. Next, you need to stop speaking about your problem and start speaking to your problem. Finally, you need to ask God for what you want or need. Jesus did not stretch out His hand to Peter until Peter asked.

1.  Which of these steps are you currently taking in any area where you are experiencing the symptoms of being overwhelmed?

_____

_____

_____

_____

_____

_____

2. Are there any of these steps you need to begin taking?

_____

_____

_____

_____

_____

_____

3. When you have a problem is your tendency to talk about it a lot? _____ If yes, how can you change that?

_____

_____

_____

_____

_____

_____

Can I challenge you to try speaking to your problem rather than about your problem? Counsel is good, but I recommend you only share problems with those who are part of the solution. I want to give you a call to action. For the next 30 days, make a covenant with your mouth to speak to your problems, thank God for the answer, and then give them to God. If you do need direction, ask yourself, "Is this person I'm about to share with part of the solution?" If not, don't share.

**Set a reminder** on your phone or calendar. Be sure to set a weekly reminder to follow up on your progress.

# **Prayer of Commitment**

Father, I ask that You help me to see my problems as opportunities. I will release them to You and speak Your Word over them and ask You for my needs. Thank You Father that You always have my best interest at heart. In Jesus' Name.

## Look Back

Since completing the call to action, are you less overwhelmed? In what ways?

_____

_____

_____

_____

_____

What will you continue to work on?

_____

_____

_____

_____

_____

# SECTION 4


# PARTICULAR ISSUES
# WE'RE OVERWHELMED
# WITH

# Chapter 14

# Overwhelmed by Emotions

## Connect with His Word

Psalm 139, Psalm 6, Romans 12:2,
Philippians 4:8

## One Minute Devotional

 It is said that the book of Psalms is for the heart. You'll find that quite often as David and the other psalmists pour out their hearts it is like they are on an emotional rollercoaster. You see this as demonstrated by the stark contrast in tone between Psalm 6 and Psalm 139, and this is just one contrasting example from the 150 psalms. From time to time, you and I can struggle with emotions that are not necessarily healthy. Welcome to the human race! I know it helps me to think that King David, a man after God's own heart, sometimes struggled with fear, depression, and other unhealthy emotions. However, you can't use David as an excuse to wallow in the pit of despair. "So how do I tame my unruly emotions?" I'm glad you asked. Romans 12:2 gives us one important key to get you off the proverbial rollercoaster.

> "Don't copy the behavior and customs of this world, but let God transform you into a new person by changing the way you think. Then you will learn to know God's will for you, which is good and pleasing and perfect." Romans 12:2 (NLT)

Most of your negative emotions begin with unrenewed thinking, because emotions are generally triggered by your thoughts. When you change your thinking, it will change your outlook and feelings. When you know God's will for you and understand it is good, pleasing, and perfect it will bring you more stability, peace, and joy.

> **Trying to manage an emotion like anger is like trying to herd cats.**

> **Depression is anger, fear, frustration, or hurt that's turned inward on oneself.**

*So Jezebel sent this message to Elijah: "May the gods strike me and even kill me if by this time tomorrow I have not killed you just as you killed them."*

*Elijah was afraid and fled for his life. He went to Beersheba, a town in Judah, and he left his servant there." 1 Kings 19:2-3 (NLT)*

# One of the first symptoms of an unhealthy emotion is you experience unhealthy fear.

Are you struggling with any unhealthy fears?

_____

_____

_____

_____

_____

_____

What?

_____

_____

_____

_____

_____

_____

## Another symptom of an unhealthy emotion is when you begin to isolate yourself.

> "Then he went on alone into the wilderness, traveling all day. He sat down under a solitary broom tree and prayed that he might die. "I have had enough, Lord," he said. "Take my life, for I am no better than my ancestors who have already died." 1 Kings 19:4 (NLT)

When you're feeling down, do you tend to isolate yourself? Why do you think you do this?

_____

_____

_____

_____

_____

_____

> **Your emotions will lie, your mind will lie, God will never lie.**

*in hope of eternal life which God, who cannot lie, promised before time began.*
*Titus 1:2 (NKJV)*

## Marker Moment

LIFE IS MEASURED BY MOMENTS

In this chapter, we get a glimpse into the life of Elijah and a time when his emotions spiraled in an unhealthy way. We saw that if we don't manage our emotions, they will manage us. Through Elijah's journey, we learned how to recognize unhealthy emotions in ourselves and understand the roots.

1. Do you recognize any of the unhealthy emotions Elijah experienced in your own life? What are they, and how are you going to deal with them?

_____

_____

_____

_____

_____

_____

_____

Emotions are directly connected to your thought life. If you're having trouble defeating negative emotions, I recommend reading *40 Days to a Joy Filled Life* by Tommy Newberry.

## Prayer of Commitment

Father, I ask You to reveal areas where I am nurturing unhealthy emotions. I will put Your Word in my mind and in my mouth. Remind me when I  think thoughts that don't glorify You and put me into an emotional downward spiral. I thank You in advance for Your help with this. In Jesus' Name. Amen.

This will be a daily Look Back so you can check in with your thought life as you are applying Romans 12:2 to your life. You will gain further tools to overcome negative emotions in the prescriptions found in the next chapter.

## Look Back

 Check your thought life daily this week. Record if you had more negative or positive thoughts each day and your most frequent thought. At the end of the week look back. What thoughts should you keep, and which ones should you dismiss?

Day 1:

_____

_____

_____

_____

_____

Day 2:

_____

_____

_____

_____

_____

Day 3:

_____

_____

_____

_____

_____

_____

Day 4:

_____

_____

_____

_____

_____

_____

Day 5:

_____

_____

_____

_____

_____

_____


Day 6:

_____

_____

_____

_____

_____

Day 7:

_____

_____

_____

_____

_____

Keep:

_____

_____

_____

_____

_____

Dismiss:

_____

_____

_____

_____

_____


What will you continue to work on?

_____

_____

_____

_____

_____

# Chapter 15

# RX for Emotional Overload

## Connect with His Word

Psalm 122, Hebrews 10 (NLT)

## One Minute Devotional

When I was a young, I remember a song we used to sing almost every week at the little church we attended. It went, "Let us go, let us go, let us go into the house of the Lord. We will praise His name, we will worship the Lord together." There is just something about gathering with a bunch of fellow believers and worshipping God together that can't be replicated in a solo experience. The writer of Hebrews 10:25 (NLT) strongly exhorts us to not neglect meeting together. One of the enemy's most successful tactics is to get you isolated from the encouragement of other believers. That's how predators operate, they pick off the stragglers. There is strength in numbers. When your emotions are overwhelming you, sometimes it is counter-intuitive to run toward people when we're feeling down, because isolation feels safe. That's the lie, isolation is the enemy's trap. Next time you're tempted to isolate, choose to surround yourself with faith-filled people who love you—the body of Christ.

> *"Then he lay down and slept under the broom tree. But as he was sleeping, an angel touched him and told him, 'Get up and eat!'" 1 Kings 19:5 (NLT)*

> **If you'll take every question mark and replace it with a plus sign, you'll see a cross.**

When your emotions are out of control, is your first instinct to take it to God?

_____

_____

_____

_____

_____

_____

_____

If not, where is your first go-to?

_____

_____

_____

_____

_____

_____

Why?

_____

_____

_____

_____

_____

_____

*"There he came to a cave, where he spent the night. But the Lord said to him, "What are you doing here, Elijah?"*

*Elijah replied, "I have zealously served the Lord God Almighty. But the people of Israel have broken their covenant with you, torn down your altars, and killed every one of your prophets. I am the only one left, and now they are trying to kill me, too." 1 Kings 19:9-10 (NLT)*

> **God loves you wherever you are, and He loves you so much, He won't leave you there.**

*"Then he lay down and slept under the broom tree." 1 Kings 19:5a (NLT)*

*"So Moses brought Israel from the Red Sea; then they went out into the Wilderness of Shur. And they went three days in the wilderness and found no water. Now when they came to Marah, they could not drink the waters of Marah, for they were bitter. Therefore the name of it was called Marah. And the people complained against Moses, saying, 'What shall we drink?' So he cried out to the Lord, and the Lord showed him a tree. When he cast it into the waters, the waters were made sweet." Exodus 15:22-25 (NKJV)*

# RX #1: Sleep.

> **One of the most practical things you will do to help stabilize your life emotionally is to build a healthy rhythm where you rest.**

Do you make getting adequate rest a priority? If you're not getting enough rest, how can you rearrange your schedule to accommodate your rest needs?

_____

_____

_____

_____

_____

_____

*"Then as he lay and slept under a broom tree, suddenly an angel touched him, and said to him, 'Arise and eat.' Then he looked, and there by his head was a cake baked on coals, and a jar of*

*water. So he ate and drank, and lay down again. And the angel of the Lord came back the second time, and touched him, and said, 'Arise and eat, because the journey is too great for you.' So he arose, and ate and drank; and he went in the strength of that food forty days and forty nights as far as Horeb, the mountain of God." 1 Kings 19:5-8 (NKJV)*

# RX #2: Church.

*Not forsaking the assembling of ourselves together, as is the manner of some, but exhorting one another, and so much the more as you see the Day approaching. Hebrews 10:25 (NKJV)*

> **The reason you're struggling is because you're filling your life with more of what the world says, than what the Word of God says.**

Is church an option or a must for your family? Why?

_____

_____

_____

_____

_____

_____

> *"And there he went into a cave, and spent the night in that place; and behold, the word of the Lord came to him, and He said to him, "What are you doing here, Elijah?" 1 Kings 19:9 (NKJV)*

# RX #3: God challenges it.

> *"So he said, "I have been very zealous for the Lord God of hosts; for the children of Israel have forsaken Your covenant, torn down Your altars, and killed Your prophets with the sword. I alone am left; and they seek to take my life." 1 Kings 19:10 (NKJV)*

> **You can't tame what you can't name.**

> **Inside depression, it can always be traced back to a lie that was believed.**

If you are experiencing depression, ask the Lord what lie you have believed. What is that lie?

_____

_____

_____

_____

_____

_____

*"And you shall know the truth, and the truth shall make you free." John 8:32 (NKJV)*

## RX #4: Now that we named it, we can change it.

*"Yet I have reserved seven thousand in Israel, all whose knees have not bowed to Baal, and every mouth that has not kissed him." 1 Kings 19:18 (NKJV)*

> **Everyone needs a friend who will say, "Hey, I love you, but that's wrong."**

Who is that friend who loves you enough to tell you the truth?

_____

_____

_____

_____

_____

_____

*"Faithful are the wounds of a friend, But the kisses of an enemy are deceitful." Proverbs 27:6 (NKJV)*

> **Circumstances begin to feed us lies, and if we're not careful, we believe them.**

*"Before I formed you in the womb I knew you, before you were born I set you apart;" Jeremiah 1:5a (NIV)*

*". . . .be transformed by the renewing of your mind, that you may prove what is that good and acceptable and perfect will of God." Romans 12:2b (NKJV)*

*"Finally brothers, whatever is true, whatever is honorable, whatever is just, whatever is pure, whatever is lovely, whatever is commendable—if there is any moral excellence and if there is any praise—dwell on these things." Philippians 4:8 (Holman)*

> **We are to dwell on the truth, and what is good and right.**

What do you allow your mind to dwell on most of the time?

_____

_____

_____

_____

_____

_____

> **You can't stop feelings from coming, but you can keep them from staying.**

> **Feelings are not the facts. God's Word is the fact that supersedes whatever it is you feel.**

> **As I replace what I feel with what I believe, what I believe will change what I feel.**

*"Then the Lord said to him: "Go, return on your way to the Wilderness of Damascus; and when you arrive, anoint Hazael as king over Syria. Also you shall anoint Jehu the son of Nimshi as king over Israel. And Elisha the son of Shaphat of Abel Meholah you shall anoint as prophet in your place. 1 Kings 19:15-16 (NKJV)*

# RX #5: Transform it.

> **The fastest way out of self-pity and depression is to get your eyes off yourself and start serving someone else.**

Who can you serve today?

_____

_____

_____

_____

_____

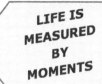

## Marker Moment

In this chapter, we discussed one of the most common emotional struggles people in our culture deal with, and that's depression. We saw from the life of Elijah five prescriptions to beat depression. Depression often is the result of believing lies as opposed to God's truth. Thoughts produce feelings, and as I replace what I feel with God's truth, what I believe will change what I feel. A key thought was feelings are not facts. God's Word is the fact that supersedes whatever it is that you feel.

1. Are there lies you've been believing that contradict what God says? If so, what are they?

_____

_____

_____

_____

_____

2.   What truths will you replace them with?

_____

_____

_____

_____

_____

_____

3.   Make a list of scriptures that tell you who you are in Christ and keep it visible. Commit one of these scriptures to memory each week and speak them out loud, especially when you're tempted to entertain the lies again.

_____

_____

_____

_____

_____

4.  Review the 5 RX for depression each week when you Look Back to make sure you're staying on track.

## Prayer of Commitment

Father, today I choose to dwell on who You say I am and not what my thoughts or feelings are telling me. Thank You for sending godly friends into my life who will come alongside me and love me enough to tell me the truth. Show me from Your word who I am in You. Please remind me if I slip and start to let those wrong thinking and believing patterns into my mind and heart. In Jesus' Name. Amen.

**Set a reminder** on your phone or calendar to look back weekly and monitor your progress out of the grip of depression.

## Look Back

Now that you are actively replacing lies with the truth, how has that affected your emotions? Has your joy level increased?

_____

_____

_____

_____

_____

What will you continue to work on?

_____

_____

_____

_____

_____

# Chapter 16

# Overwhelmed by Lack

## Connect with His Word

Matthew 25, Luke 19 (NLT)

## One Minute Devotional

Have you ever had a windfall where you got some unexpected money or a tax refund and without praying you rushed out to buy something extravagant you'd been wanting? Then, lo and behold a few days later the car broke down, or the washer quit, and the cost of the repair was the amount of your windfall? I think most of us have learned that lesson the hard way. God is more concerned about your stewardship like the stories in our Bible reading. When you realize everything that comes into your hands is a gift from God and that He is trusting you to be a steward, it will change everything. That's why you tithe, you're saying God I honor You as my provider. When you see God as your provider, it changes the way you view your money. All you have is on loan from God; it's a test to see what He can trust you with in eternity.

*"The thief does not come except to steal, and to kill, and to destroy. I have come that they may have life, and that they may have it more abundantly." John 10:10 (NKJV)*

*"And my God shall supply all your need according to His riches in glory by Christ Jesus." Philippians 4:19 (NKJV)*

**In this life however, we still encounter seasons of lack from time to time.**

*"These things I have spoken to you, that in Me you may have peace. In the world you will have tribulation; but be of good cheer, I have overcome the world." John 16:33 (NKJV)*

*"Now it came to pass, in the days when the judges ruled, that there was a famine in the land. And a certain man of Bethlehem, Judah, went to dwell in the country of Moab, he and his wife and his two sons." Ruth 1:1 (NKJV)*

> **We go into battle with praise, because praise requires us to use faith and it releases the power of God on our behalf.**

*"Moab is My washpot;*
*Over Edom I will cast My shoe;*
*Over Philistia I will triumph." Psalm 108:9 (NKJV)*

*"Then Elimelech, Naomi's husband, died; and she was left, and her two sons." Ruth 1:3 (NKJV)*

*"Now they took wives of the women of Moab: the name of the one was Orpah, and the name of the other Ruth. And they dwelt there about ten years. Then both Mahlon and Chilion also died; so the woman survived her two sons and her husband." Ruth 1:4-5 (NKJV)*

> **Here's what happens when we as parents go to the world, it affects our kids.**

In light of this chapter, what are you modeling to your kids?

_____

_____

_____

_____

_____

_____

# 1. Realize leaving leads to loss.

*"I went out full, and the Lord has brought me home again empty." Ruth 1:21a (NKJV)*

> **Know this, your worst day in God's house is better than the best day the world has to offer.**

*"Then she arose with her daughters-in-law that she might return from the country of Moab, for she had heard in the country of Moab that the Lord had visited His people by giving them bread.*

*Therefore she went out from the place where she was, and her two daughters-in-laws with her; and they went on the way to return to the land of Judah."*
*Ruth 1:6-7 (NKJV)*

> **When you realize you're living in a toilet bowl, your first step is to return to the Bread of Life, Jesus.**

# 2. Acknowledge you need to return.

> **He's King of Kings, not the God of, "Have it your way."**

Have you been guilty of trying to have it your way instead of God's way? How?

_____

_____

_____

_____

_____

*"But godliness with contentment is great gain. For we brought nothing into the world, and we can take nothing out of it. But if we have food and clothing, we will be content with that. Those who want to get rich fall into temptation and a trap and into many foolish and harmful desires that plunge people into ruin and destruction. For the love of money is a root of all kinds of evil. Some people, eager for money, have wandered from the faith and pierced themselves with many griefs."* 1 Timothy 6:6-11 (NIV)

> **When we seek to find our value and identity in material things, we're setting ourselves up for grief.**

> **The reality is, every one of us can probably find some-where in our life, where we're not surrendered to God's Word.**

# 3. Make a commitment to return.

*So, the two women went on until they came to Bethlehem. When they arrived in Bethlehem, the whole town was stirred because of them, and the women exclaimed, "Can this be Naomi?" Ruth 1:19 (NIV)*

*"Then they lifted up their voices and wept again; and Orpah kissed her mother-in-law, but Ruth clung to her. And she said, "Look, your sister-in-law has gone back to her people and to her gods; return after your sister-in-law." But Ruth said: "Entreat me not to leave you, Or to turn back from following after you; For wherever you go, I will go; And wherever you lodge, I will lodge; Your people shall be my people, And your God, my God. Where you die, I will die, And there will I be buried. The Lord do so to me, and more also, If anything but death parts you and me." Ruth 1:14-17 (NKJV)*

# 4. When you return, there are some things you have to release.

> **What is it that you need to leave behind?**

# 5. When you return, there are some things you retain.

> **Wisdom is learning from other people's experiences.**

*"Therefore I say to you, her sins, which are many, are forgiven, for she loved much. But to whom little is forgiven, the same loves little." Luke 7: 47-48 (NKJV)*

> **It's not how much Bible you know, but how much Bible you live that counts.**

An honest heart search moment: Are there areas where you know the Word, but you're not living it? What areas?

_____

_____

_____

_____

_____

_____

> *"But knowledge puffs up while love builds up." 1 Corinthians 8:1b (NIV)*

# 6. When you return, there are things you need to pick up.

> *"There was a relative of Naomi's husband, a man of great wealth, of the family of Elimelech. His name was Boaz. So Ruth the Moabitess said to Naomi, "Please let me go to the field, and glean heads of grain after him in whose sight I may find favor."*

> *And she said to her, "Go, my daughter."*

*Then she left, and went and gleaned in the field after the reapers. And she happened to come to the part of the field belonging to Boaz, who was of the family of Elimelech." Ruth 2:1-3 (NKJV)*

*Then Boaz said to Ruth, "You will listen, my daughter, will you not? Do not go to glean in another field, nor go from here, but stay close by my young women. Let your eyes be on the field which they reap, and go after them. Have I not commanded the young men not to touch you? And when you are thirsty, go to the vessels and drink from what the young men have drawn."*

*So she fell on her face, bowed down to the ground, and said to him, "Why have I found favor in your eyes, that you should take notice of me, since I am a foreigner?"*

*And Boaz answered and said to her, "It has been fully reported to me, all that you have done for your mother-in-law since the death of your husband, and how you have left your father and your mother and the land of your birth, and have come to a people whom you did not know before. The Lord repay your work, and a full reward be given you by the Lord God of Israel, under whose wings you have come for refuge." Ruth 2:8-12 (NKJV)*

*"Do you not say, 'There are still four months and then comes the harvest?' Behold, I say to you, lift up your eyes and look at the fields, for they are already white for harvest!" John 4:35 (NKJV)*

> **When you come back, no matter how far you've wandered, you're part of God's family.**

**LIFE IS MEASURED BY MOMENTS**

## Marker Moment

In this chapter, we talked about lack through the lens of the book of Ruth. We saw the detriment of going to the world to try to get your needs met or find your identity, and the value in doing things God's way.

1. Are there any areas in your life where you're experiencing lack? If so, what areas?

_____

_____

_____

_____

_____

2. Are there any areas that you're finding yourself living the world's way? What areas?

_____

_____

_____

_____

_____

3. Are there any correlations between the lack you're experiencing and the areas in which you're

following the world? If yes, which ones? How can you get on track?

_____

_____

_____

_____

_____

_____

**Set a reminder** on your phone or calendar weekly so you can track your progress. Write your progress or regressions down. Do remember what you write down.

# Prayer of Commitment

Lord, please forgive me for attempting to get my needs met from the world. I commit to follow Your ways. Help me to follow You in every area of my life. In Jesus' Name. Amen.

## Look Back

 Now that you're getting your life back on track, how have things changed? Keep looking back on a regular basis. Remember to express your gratitude to God on a regular basis.

_____

_____

_____

_____

What will you continue to work on?

_____

_____

_____

_____

_____

# Chapter 17

# Finding A Vision

## Connect with His Word

Proverbs 29, Luke 14:25-35

## One Minute Devotional

 Proverbs 29:11 (KJV) tells us, *"Without a vision the people perish."* Vision gives you direction and adds definition to your life. Without a vision you're figuratively in the middle of the ocean in a rowboat without a paddle. Vision is your paddle to get you where God wants you to go. Vision helps you avoid the proverbial icebergs of life. If you haven't spent time with the Lord seeking His vision for your life, I encourage you to do just that. When you have a vision, it frees you from distractions. You are not guaranteed a wave-free life, but when you have a vision, you'll be able to navigate the storms of life and arrive safely at your God appointed destination.

> **More money will not solve your problem until your vision for your money is bigger than what you currently have.**

*"Where there is no vision, the people perish" Proverbs 29:18a (KJV)*

> **"God give me a vision for my life that's greater than living for the moment."**

*"Then one of them, a lawyer, asked Him a question, testing Him, and saying, 'Teacher, which is the great commandment in the law?'"*

*Jesus said to him, "'You shall love the Lord your God with all your heart, with all your soul, and with all your mind.' This is the first and great commandment. And the second is like it: 'You shall love your neighbor as yourself.' On these two commandments hang all the Law and the Prophets." Matthew 22:35-40 (NKJV)*

> So, if you're a Christ
> follower, Jesus already
> defined your mission for you,
> love God and love people.

# #1. God has a vision for your life.

> If you're praying and getting
> crickets, it might be because
> you have a vision that's
> different from God's vision.

*"I will stand my watch
And set myself on the rampart,
And watch to see what He will say to
me,
And what I will answer when I am
corrected." Habakkuk 2:1 (NKJV)*

*"Then the Lord answered me and said:
"Write the vision
And make it plain on tablets,
That he may run who reads it."
Habakkuk 2:2 (NKJV)*

There are five areas that you need God's vision for in your life.

1. Your faith.

2. Your family.

3. Your fitness.

4. Your finances.

5. Your field of occupation.

*"For I know the plans I have for you,"* says the Lord. *"They are plans for good and not for disaster, to give you a future and a hope. In those days when you pray, I will listen. If you look for me wholeheartedly, you will find me."* Jeremiah 29:11-13 (NLT)

*"Ask, and it will be given to you; seek, and you will find; knock, and it will be opened to you."* Matthew 7:7 (NKJV)

## #2. Start with the end in mind.

*"Oh, that they were wise, that they understood this, that they would consider their latter end!"* Deuteronomy 32:29 (NKJV)

## #3. You need to write down what God tells you.

## #4. Keep it simple.

*"Well done good and faithful servant."*
*Matthew 25:23b (NIV)*

> **If I win the entire world to Christ, but fail with my family, then I have failed in my highest calling.**

> **You can't take it with you, but you can send it ahead of you!**

*"Then the Lord answered me and said:*
*"Write the vision*
*And make it plain on tablets,*
*That he may run who reads it."*
*Habakkuk 2:2 (NKJV)*

> **Remember, you keep valuable what you keep visible.**

*LIFE IS MEASURED BY MOMENTS*

## Marker Moment

In this chapter, we discovered that most of our problems are due to a lack of vision. We saw we need two things to help keep us on track to achieve the life God created us to have. We need a mission statement and a vision statement. We also need a vision for the five most important areas of our lives.

1. My mission statement is:

_____

_____

_____

_____

_____

2. My vision statement is:

_____

_____

_____

_____

_____

_____

3. My vision statements for the five pillars of my life are:

Faith:

_____

_____

_____

_____

_____

_____

Family:

_____

_____

_____

_____

_____

_____

Fitness:

_____

_____

_____

_____

_____

Finances:

_____

_____

_____

_____

_____

Field of Occupation:

_____

_____

_____

_____

_____

## Prayer of Commitment

Father, I pray for Your direction in getting the mission and vision statement for my life. Help me to choose Your will for my life and not what I just think it should be. I ask for guidance in developing direction for these five key areas so my life will line up with Your mission and vision for my life. In Jesus' Name. Amen.

## Look Back

Make a copy of your vision, mission statements and your five pillars and make it a habit to look over them daily.

# Chapter 18

# Goals

## Connect with His Word

Psalm 91, Proverbs 16

## One Minute Devotional

 Setting goals is sort of like archery. You have arrows, a bow, and a target with a bullseye in the middle. The whole point is to put your arrow in the bow, pull it back, and then have that arrow fly through the air and hopefully hit the bullseye. If you want to hit the bullseye with your goals, start with seeking God for His direction for your life. If you're like me, you've probably had some brilliant ideas that you just took off running with without even asking God if that was His direction for you. That kind of plan seldom hits the bullseye. Seek God in all you do, and He will show you which path to take. God hits the bullseye every time.

# Setting Goals

> *"And He was handed the book of the prophet Isaiah. And when He had opened the book, He found the place where it was written:*
>
> *"The Spirit of the Lord is upon Me, Because He has anointed Me To preach the gospel to the poor; He has sent Me to heal the brokenhearted, To proclaim liberty to the captives And recovery of sight to the blind, To set at liberty those who are oppressed;*
>
> *To proclaim the acceptable year of the Lord."*
>
> *Then He closed the book, and gave it back to the attendant and sat down." Luke 4:17-20a (NKJV)*

Jesus came predominantly to do five things. These defined His vision.

> *"but the people who know their God shall be strong, and carry out great exploits." Daniel 11:32b (NKJV)*

*"I have come that they may have life, and that they may have it more abundantly." John 10:10b (NKJV)*

*"He left Judea and departed again to Galilee. But He needed to go through Samaria." John 4:3-4 (NKJV)*

# 1. Your goals need to be in writing.

*"Write down this vision;*
*clearly inscribe it on tablets*
*so one may easily read it." Habakkuk 2:2b (Holman)*

# 2. Your goals need to be measurable.

**You can't manage what you can't measure.**

# 3. Your goals should be broken into steps.

> *"The steps of a good man are ordered by the Lord,*
> *And He delights in his way." Psalm 37:23 (NKJV)*

> *"And He said to them, "Why did you seek Me? Did you not know that I must be about My Father's business?" Luke 2:49 (NKJV)*

# 4. Your goals need a deadline.

> *"Brothers, I do not consider myself to have taken hold of it. But one thing I do: Forgetting what is behind and reaching forward to what is ahead, I pursue as my goal the prize promised by God's heavenly call in Christ Jesus." Philippians 3:13-14 (Holman)*

# 5. Your goals should be reviewed regularly.

> *"For which of you, intending to build a tower, does not sit down first and count*

*the cost, whether he has enough to finish it" Luke 14:28 (NKJV)*

LIFE IS
MEASURED
BY
MOMENTS

## Marker Moment

In this chapter, we found your goals are your roadmap to achieving your vision. These goals must be in writing, be measurable, broken into steps, have a deadline, and be reviewed regularly to check progress, then adjusted as needed. Use this space to set some goals for a specific area of your vision.

Goals: List them on the next pages.

1. _____

_____

_____

_____

_____

Deadline: _____.

2. _____

_____

_____

_____

_____

MONTH _____ YEAR _____

Deadline: _____.

3. _____

_____

_____

_____

_____

MONTH _____ YEAR _____

Deadline: _____.

4. _____

_____

_____

_____

_____

MONTH _____ YEAR _____

Deadline: _____.

5. _____

_____

_____

_____

_____

| MONTH | | | YEAR | | | |
|---|---|---|---|---|---|---|

Deadline: _____.

If you have goals for other areas, use this format on a separate paper.

## Prayer of Commitment

Father, help me have a life of order and discipline. Your word tells us in Proverbs that these are the people who prosper. I choose to pursue Your highest  and best for my life. In Jesus' Name. Amen.

# Look Back

 Make a copy of your goals and make it a habit to look over them daily.

# Chapter 19
# Final Thoughts

## Connect with His Word

Proverbs 18

## One Minute Devotional

 There is a renowned author and speaker named Andy Andrews. He grew up in a Christian home. His father was a minister of music, and his mom played the piano and organ and directed the choir. At the age of 19, Andy tragically lost both of his parents within a few months span, his mother from cancer and his father in an automobile accident. These loses put Andy into a tailspin and he ended up homeless and living under a peer on a beach in Alabama. While there, a man befriended him who shared with him the value of reading the biographies of great historical figures. He ended up reading over 200. These books inspired him to develop the seven decisions that led him to write his first best-selling novel.

There are two things that will change your life, what you read and your relationships. For Andy, God provided a friend to help guide him to the books he needed to inspire him to his God-given destiny. Do you have people in your life to inspire you to your God-given destiny? Do you consistently fill your heart and mind with books that will inspire you to higher things?

*"If the ax is dull,*
*And one does not sharpen the edge,*
*Then he must use more strength;*
*But   wisdom   brings   success."*
*Ecclesiastes 10:10 (NKJV)*

> **The right question is not, what do I need to do, it's who do I need to become?**

*"In the course of time, there was another battle with the Philistines, at Gob. At that time Sibbekai the Hushathite killed Saph, one of the descendants of Rapha. In another battle with the Philistines at Gob, Elhanan son of Jair the Bethlehemite killed the brother of Goliath the Gittite,*

*who had a spear with a shaft like a weaver's rod.*

*In still another battle, which took place at Gath, there was a huge man with six fingers on each hand and six toes on each foot—twenty-four in all. He also was descended from Rapha. When he taunted Israel, Jonathan son of Shimeah, David's brother, killed him."* 2 Samuel 21:18-21 (NIV)

> **If you want to see change around you, you become the change you want to see. Because you reproduce what you are.**

*"Therefore, if anyone is in Christ, he is a new creation; old things have passed away; behold, all things have become new."* 2 Corinthians 5:17 (NKJV)

*"But God, who is rich in mercy, because of His great love with which He loved us, even when we were dead in trespasses, made us alive together with Christ (by grace you have been saved), and raised us up together, and made us*

*sit together in the heavenly places in
Christ Jesus," Ephesians 2:4-6 (NKJV)*

*"For we are God's masterpiece. He has
created us anew in Christ Jesus, so we
can do the good things he planned for
us long ago." Ephesians 2:10 (NLT)*

> **What you believe will change
> how you behave.**

Does my behavior reflect what I say my beliefs are?
If not, what do I need to change?

_____

_____

_____

_____

_____

> **Here are those two simple things that will change your life: what you read and your relationships.**

# First, what are you reading?

*"This Book of the Law shall not depart from your mouth, but you shall meditate in it day and night, that you may observe to do according to all that is written in it. For then you will make your way prosperous, and then you will have good success." Joshua 1:8 (NKJV)*

# Second, your relationships.

*Walk with the wise and become wise, for a companion of fools suffers harm. Proverbs 13:20 (NIV)*

*"And everyone who was in distress, everyone who was in debt, and everyone who was discontented gathered to him. So he became captain over them. And there were about four hundred men with him." 1 Samuel 22:2 (NKJV)*

> **You'll rise or fall to the level of your relationships.**

> **The crowd will never change the world, it's the committed few who are willing to make the climb.**

*Be very careful, then, how you live—not as unwise but as wise, making the most of every opportunity, because the days are evil. Ephesians 5:15-16 (NIV)*

> **We need to learn the power of no.**

*"Someone in the crowd said to him, "Teacher, tell my brother to divide the inheritance with me." Jesus replied, "Man, who appointed me a judge or an arbiter between you?" Luke 12:13-14 (NIV)*

*"I'm the true vine. My father is the vinedresser. Every branch in Me that does not bear fruit he takes away and every branch that bears fruit He*

*prunes, that it may bear more fruit."*
*John 15:1 (NKJV)*

> **How you decide to use your time will determine your legacy.**

## LIFE IS MEASURED BY MOMENTS

## Marker Moment

This chapter centered around a profound statement, "Before I can have, I must do, and before I do, I must become." To reach God's best and highest is instead about who we become. Who you become is largely dependent on what you read and your relationships. Our life consists of time, when we're out of time, we're out of life. With this, we learned the importance of saying no to the wrong things, so we have the margin for the things that will bring us closer to our purpose. How we handle our time will determine our legacy.

1.    What are you currently reading?

_____

_____

_____

_____

_____


2.    What will you commit to reading to enrich your life?

_____

_____

_____

_____

MONTH            YEAR

When will you commit to do that? On (date): _____.

3. Are there relationships in your life which may be holding you back from God's highest and best for you? Who are they, and how can you lovingly back away from that relationship?

_____

_____

_____

_____

_____

4. Who do you admire that you will connect with in the next week?

_____

_____

_____

_____

_____

5.  Using your vision statement and goals are there some things you need to say "no" to because they will keep you from God's highest and best?

_____

_____

_____

_____

_____

**Set a reminder** on your phone or calendar to notify yourself to Look Back each month to see your progress and the life change you've experienced. Be sure to write down your before and after so you can see the contrast between your starting point and where you are now.

## Prayer of Commitment

God, help me to stop and listen to You before the next time I say, "yes" to the things that keep me from You. Help me always to choose those things  which will bring me closer to the vision and purpose You've given me for my life. Show me any activities or relationships that are holding me back from your highest and best. I surrender my life to You and ask You to make me who You designed me to be. In Jesus' Name. Amen.

## Look Back

 Every month after you've implemented these changes, look back over this page and reflect on the changes you have seen.

Where I was:

_____

_____

_____

_____

Where I am now:

_____

_____

_____

_____

_____

_____

What will you continue to work on?

_____

_____

_____

_____

_____

_____

# References

https://creativecommons.org/licenses/by/3.0/

# Resources

*All Out Leadership* podcast

https://eriklawson.com

Element Church website

elementchurch.com

Facebook

https://www.facebook.com/erikjlawson/

Book Erik for a speaking engagement.

Pastor Erik is available for speaking engagements, leadership coaching, and church consulting. He speaks on leadership, church development, and peak performance with a practical, creative, and humorous delivery that entertains and inspires. Use the link below and go to the resource page to get information on his availability for your event, or to get more information.

https://eriklawson.com

# About the Author

Erik Lawson is the founding pastor of Element Church, a congregation of more than 5,000 with its main campus located in Wentzville, Missouri. He is known for his dynamic communication style and in-depth Bible teaching communicated with practical life application. In addition to his role as the senior pastor of a multi-site local church, and a world-wide online presence with Element Everywhere, he has an insightful leadership podcast called *All Out Leadership* and is a one-on-one leadership coach to pastors.

Prior to founding Element Church he led what was at the time, the largest youth group in America, Church on The Move's nationally acclaimed,

Oneighty©, with as many as 3,000 young people attending each week.

Erik lives in Wentzville, Missouri with his wife Sunny and their dog Flash. He is the father of three wonderful adult children and has two beautiful granddaughters. In his free time, Erik enjoys spending time reading, playing Fortnite with friends, going for walks in the park with Sunny, and eating ice cream.

Made in the USA
Monee, IL
27 January 2023

26431308R00134